Dear Dave & Wife

I hope

my b

Best Wishes,

[signature]

31-95-17

April's Pond

I.J. Lyons

authorHOUSE®

AuthorHouse™ UK Ltd.
500 Avebury Boulevard
Central Milton Keynes, MK9 2BE
www.authorhouse.co.uk
Phone: 08001974150

© 2009 I.J. Lyons. All rights reserved.

No part of this book may be reproduced, stored in a retrieval system, or transmitted by any means without the written permission of the author.

First published by AuthorHouse 10/14/2009

ISBN: 978-1-4490-3066-7 (sc)

Library of Congress Control Number: 2009909810

This book is printed on acid-free paper.

Contents

1. Alien Sunday — 1
2. Hedge Pig — 9
3. The Garden — 14
4. Pond Life — 24
5. Lost and Found — 32
6. Practice Makes Permanent — 39
7. A Nice Surprise — 43
8. Let the Show Begin! — 47
9. Encore — 51
10. A Party to Remember — 55
11. The Revelation — 59
12. Boar Meets Sow — 63
13. Destiny — 66

Chapter 1 - Alien Sunday

'Where are you going in such a hurry?' asked Hannah.

'The gang have captured an alien,' said Robert, 'they told me on the walkie-talkie. I'm on my way to the Del now.'

'Don't be silly. Aliens don't exist!'

But Robert was already out of the front door.

'Hannah, come in here and eat your breakfast,' her mother shouted from the kitchen, 'and fetch your brother too!'

Hannah went to the kitchen; it smelt of bacon, coffee, and lemon from the cleaned table. It had the look and feel of a farmhouse kitchen that Mrs Watt had long desired, and Mr Watt had worked hard to create for her.

Hannah picked up a slice of toast but dropped it on the floor. She quickly put it back on her plate before her mother noticed. 'Robert went to the Del.'

'This early? Well, go and fetch him; he's not playing out on an empty stomach.'

Hannah's father Mr Watt wandered into the kitchen in search of the shed keys.

'Want my toast Dad? I have to go looking for Robert.'

'Thanks, that'd be grand!' he said, taking a bite from the dropped slice.

Hannah said nothing and scurried out the back door with a cheeky grin.

The dash through the backyard and down Smugglers Lane left Hannah short of breath in the day's heat.

Keeping track of Robert's activities was a task she often had to endure. It was an inconvenience, but it provided the opportunity to meet some of his older friends who often paid attention to her.

A thorn scratched her arm as she squeezed through the hole in the bush to enter the Del. It was a triangular wooded area of no man's land between three properties with one dominant tree at the centre. The place had a fresh and exciting smell as if ancient battles had been fought there between heroes and dragons. It smelled of old, crispy, brown leaves and the ashes of a stone fireplace.

'Who goes there?' shouted Robert from the tree house.

'It's Hannah, can I come up?'

'Absolutely not!' said a voice from somewhere higher in the tree. 'You don't even know the password.'

'And even if you did, we wouldn't let you because you're a girl,' said another voice, which Hannah recognized as Adam Clown, one of the boys in her class.

'We have an Alien prisoner up here and we can't have just anyone poking their noses around it,' shouted Robert.

Hannah sighed and said, 'I couldn't care less about your pretend alien. Mum said you have to come home for breakfast.'

She *was* curious to find out what was going on, but pretended not to care.

A rope ladder dropped from the tree house and nearly hit Hannah on the head. Robert climbed down and brushed the green dirt from his trousers with his hand. 'See you later guys. You're in charge of the Alien while I'm away.'

As they climbed back through the hole in the bush, Adam secretly watched Hannah leave and smiled.

He had noticed Robert's sister before, but now saw her in a different light. She seemed to have grown up quickly in the last year, and, although younger than him, she was very mature for her age. Whenever she was around, he always found himself taking the role of a knight in shining armour to impress her and often succeeded.

Mrs Watt put a pitcher of orange juice on the table, just as the children returned to the kitchen. Robert didn't waste any time and tucked into the spread of food on the table.

'Just exactly what is the rush Robert?' asked Mrs Watt, as he began spooning the cereal into his mouth as fast as he could.

'We're executing the alien this morning, and I still have to make the noose,' he declared.

This made no sense to anyone, which was not unusual, and Mrs Watt, typically, refused to acknowledge his wild imagination.

'Well, if you can't execute your breakfast a little slower, you'll end up feeling sick like your father.'

'Ignore him Mum. *Aliens* don't even exist,' said Hannah.

'If you don't believe me,' he said, sharply. 'Come and see for yourself. The execution will take place at 12 noon sharp.'

A horrid sound of vomiting came from the downstairs toilet followed by a flush. Mr Watt emerged and came into the kitchen looking very pale.

The last time he felt this ill, he had to be taken to hospital. He had eaten a cake the children had made for him with garden insects as ingredients.

'Here drink this,' said Mrs Watt, handing him a glass of water.

'*Ta* very much. Not poisoned is it?'

Hannah blushed and left the table, avoiding her father's eyes.

Just before twelve, the rain that had been going on for the last hour gave way to clear blue skies. Everything in the Del had been soaking wet, but dried almost instantly due to the summer heat.

Hannah pushed through the hole in the bush and looked up to the tree house to see Robert tying a thin noose made of string to one of the branches.

'Don't make it too long,' suggested Adam, 'or you'll pull its head off.'

'Pull what's head off?' shouted Hannah, confused.

'The alien of course!' he replied.

'But they don't…' began Hannah, and then stared in disbelief as Robert put his noose around a little hedgehog's neck.

The hedgehog seemed totally unaware of the two boy's intentions, happy in fact. He looked down at Hannah and seemed to be enjoying all the attention and fuss.

'Don't *you* dare!' shrieked Hannah. 'That's not an alien, it's a hedgehog.'

'It's an alien *disguised* as a hedgehog, and they're everywhere,' declared Robert.

'Robert! This has gone far enough. If you don't release that poor hedgehog I'll tell Mum about the pet snake hidden in your room.'

Robert thought for a second. He certainly didn't want his pet snake discovered, but *loved* to see his sister getting so upset about something. He had already decided not to kill the hedgehog, but continued to tease her and pretended to drop the hedgehog. 'Why do you care so much about some stupid hedgehog anyway? It's only a bit of fun.'

Hannah looked again at the adorable little animal; it was no bigger than Robert's hand. It had black eyes like tiny marbles, cute miniature ears no bigger than Hannah's thumb, and a wet nose just like a puppy dog. 'How could you think about harming this defenceless animal?'

Adam took the hedgehog carefully from Robert and climbed down to Hannah. He had found himself playing the hero again but wasn't sure what he wanted to gain from it. 'Here you go then Hannah. *You* take care of him.'

She smiled and wrapped him in her scarf, so he wouldn't get scared, and took him back to the house before they changed their mind.

Mrs Watt was sitting in the kitchen having coffee and biscuits with her close friend Mrs Robinson; Mr Watt was busy fixing a kitchen cupboard.

Mrs Robinson often visited the house and talked endlessly about the latest upgrade to her furniture or creation in the garden. She was incredibly house-proud and a little snobbish, but Mrs Watt enjoyed her company regardless. Mrs Robinson said, 'I see Hannah's found a new friend,'

Hannah held up the spiky creature and then waited with a cheeky grin of excitement for her mother's reaction. Mrs Watt was terrified of spiders, mice, and dogs. But she had never heard of anyone being scared of hedgehogs. 'I have an extra guest for lunch Mum.'

'What's that!' she demanded as Hannah put the hedgehog on the kitchen floor. 'I expect you want to keep it too?'

'Just while it's little,' said Hannah. 'It won't be any trouble, I promise.'

Mr Watt put down his tools and studied the hedgehog carefully, perhaps assessing its ability to scare his wife. He always found it difficult to disappoint Hannah, much more than Robert, but he had to appear firm. The look of joy on her face, which melted his heart, was always worthy of a compromise. He melted, 'Well, it can't be any more trouble than our Robert. But *only* while it's small, mind you.'

'You won't regret it,' she said. 'I'll take great care of him.'

Mrs Watt sensed an opportunity to develop Hannah's maternal instincts. Both she and Mr Watt tried to give the children experiences which would help them later in life. 'Well then,' she said. 'I guess you had better give the hedgehog some lunch.'

'What do they eat?' asked Mrs Robinson.

'It looks like 'ar hedge pig's decided himself!' said Mr Watt.

Everyone looked over at the kitchen floor to see the hedgehog tucking into the cat's food. The hedgehog had an incredible appetite and finished almost everything in her bowl.

The black tabby cat jumped down from the side table, arched its back, and did not look amused.

Hannah spent the rest of the day playing with the hedgehog and finding out what he liked to eat. She searched the encyclopaedia under 'hedgehog' and then rummaged around in the larder to find suitable roughage.

All too soon it was time for bed. Hannah got up from the kitchen floor and left her new friend building his bed from torn-up newspapers and an old cardboard box. She walked up the stairs to her bedroom, her mind full of the day's events.

By the time Hannah reached the top of the stairs, she had a name for her new pet, picking the most appropriate she could think of. She took the name from the cat food company he loved so much.

'Milton is his name,' she said, followed by a yawn.

Hannah stretched out her arms, fell onto her bed, and began to fall asleep without bothering to undress. She laid there and thought about Milton. She adored the little hedgehog. Surely, she could convince her parents to let her keep Milton if they found him no trouble to them. She would have to find a way.

A short time later, Mr Watt walked past Hannah's room and saw she was fast asleep. He closed her window, wrapped her up in the duvet, kissed her on the forehead, and turned off the light.

Chapter 2 - Hedge Pig

Every day before school, Hannah made sure that Milton's bowl was full of hedgehog mix bought from the pet store and was cheerfully thorough with refilling his water bowl, changing his bedding, and even cleaning the bits of fluff that stuck to his feet from the kitchen floor.

While eating her breakfast, she watched adoringly while Milton explored the kitchen to find new smells. He reminded her of Robert, when he was little, exploring a new world.

Every day when Mrs Watt brought Hannah home from school in the car, she asked about Milton and what he had been up to during the day; usually he had been causing some mischief in between naps. Once, she told her, he had managed to get stuck behind the cooker, and the rescue had delayed Mrs Watt's usual hair appointment.

Milton loved seeing Hannah's face when she returned home from school to play with him. She rushed to take off her coat, and Milton paused to stare at her with happiness in his eyes. *Something is bound to spoil this*, he thought. *This is too good to be true.*

Everywhere Hannah went, Milton followed. Sometimes, when Mrs Watt wasn't looking, he sneaked up to her room and she showed him her toy collection.

One Saturday morning, the whole family – Hannah, Robert, and Mr and Mrs Watt – had taken the car to Parker's Abbey. It was a scenic countryside spot, only thirty minutes' drive from the Watt's house, next to a shallow and gentle river.

Milton had come along too and sat happily in Hannah's lap the whole journey. He was comfortable, but he couldn't quite see out of the window, and the bouncing around had made him feel queasy.

When the car arrived, there were already two dozen other families parked up on the grass next to the river. Some were playing football or Frisbee, while others were just enjoying the sun.

Robert spotted his friend Adam and ran off to play with him. They had been friends for as long as he could remember, and they never tired of inventing new games to entertain each other. Even though Adam was a couple of years older than him, it didn't seem to matter.

Milton lay on the picnic blanket beside Hannah as she put on the sun cream. He was busy investigating new smells and sniffing around Mr and Mrs Watt's legs, performing a ritual called 'anointing'. Whenever he came across a new scent, he would first lick it to make sure it wasn't a poison, give it a little nibble to get the taste of it, chew it up with some water to make froth in his mouth, and finally paste it on his spines with his tongue. This would make him smell like everything around him. It was the perfect camouflage, and if anything horrible came along they would get a nasty surprise when he curled into a ball and pricked them, because it was also a mild poison. He hoped he would never have to use it for that.

'Ooh! That tickles,' said Mrs Watt, as he licked her ankle.

'He's anointing himself,' said Hannah. 'He must think you smell nice.'

Milton wandered around the bushes searching for insects and eventually settled under a big leaf near the picnic blanket for shelter from the sun and another nap.

Mr Watt glanced across at his wife before speaking, 'He seems happy enough here. Maybe we should let him go, Hannah.'

'No!' she shrieked. 'He would be lost here, and I would never see him again.' She couldn't believe her ears and quickly scooped Milton up in her arms, like he was about to be thrown in the river. Milton was startled and bounced around as the pair ran off.

Nearby the picnic site there was a small hilltop overlooking a narrowing in the river. Hannah and Milton found Robert playing there with Adam. The two boys had stripped off to their shorts and were standing at the edge of a sheer drop into the river. The sound of the water hitting the rocks from the gentle rapids was pleasant to the ear.

'Do you think its deep enough?' asked Adam as he peered over the edge.

'I saw someone do it last time I was here. That spot there is the best.'

He pointed towards a dark pool of still water; it was surrounded by rocks that were sheltered from the fast main flow of the river. Hannah looked over the edge nervously to where he was pointing. Milton could see over the edge too and also felt nervous. He clung tighter to Hannah and curled up into a ball to pretend it wasn't happening.

Hannah shivered and said, 'It looks very cold. Are you sure it's not too high up?'

Adam glanced at Hannah; his cheeks were red because his heart was beating much faster than normal. He wiped his hands on his shorts because of the sweat, took a deep breath, exhaled, and leapt from the edge. 'Geronimo!'

The explosion of white water sounded like a loud clap as he hit the water. He surfaced a few seconds later, gasping for air, and swam to the side of the river.

'Wow!' said Robert. 'He didn't even know for sure it was deep enough.'

Hannah's eyes were wide in disbelief, and she had an astonished grin on her face. 'Isn't he brave Milton?' she said, giggling and shaking his paw.

Milton knew he could never do anything like that. When he was still very young, he had been looking for shelter with his father when they had to cross a busy road. He didn't even know what a road was. His father had been killed instantly by a passing car – right in front of him. He never had a chance to say goodbye. *Better not to take risks*, he thought.

He licked her hand and made some more ointment for his spines; he was just pleased to be in her company. He felt safe, cared for, and truly loved. He wanted that feeling to last forever.

That evening Mr and Mrs Watt, Hannah, and Milton were in the kitchen.

Mrs Watt was boiling dinner on the stove and sweating from the heat. The whole house smelt of the delicious lamb joint she was cooking in the oven. Mr Watt was opening and closing one of the cupboards, admiring his handiwork, and Milton was on the kitchen floor with Hannah playing a game – his favourite game. 'Fetch it,' she said, throwing a small berry from his food mix.

He ran as fast as he could to impress Hannah, and he caught it quickly, coming to a halt just behind Mr Watt, who, in the same moment, stepped back from the cupboard, threw his arms into the air, and lost balance, almost tripping over Milton. He regained his footing and picked up his tools, saying, 'Okay! Enough is enough!' He looked very angry. 'He has *got* to go, Hannah. Milton is a wild animal and can look after himself!'

He very rarely got upset, but when he did, he usually got what he wanted. It would be useless to try and change his mind now.

'Go and see the Robinsons,' suggested Mrs Watt, wiping her forehead. 'Mrs Robinson said just yesterday that a hedgehog in her garden would be wonderful for pest control. Then you could still visit Milton as often as you'd like.'

Before Hannah could say a word, Mrs Watt had called her friends on the telephone. Mrs Watt spoke to Mrs Robinson. Mrs Robinson spoke to Mr Robinson. Mr Robinson called back later and spoke to Mr Watt, and then Mr Watt spoke to Mrs Watt.

The matter was settled; the next day Milton was taken to live in a rough patch at the bottom of the Robinson's garden.

Chapter 3 - The Garden

The Robinson's house was a short walk, and just a few streets away. It was made with old stone and had ivy creeping up to a nesting box for the house martins. The shortest route was down the bramble-lined path of Smuggler's Lane.

The garden was almost the size of a football pitch – a little thinner and longer and without goalposts. It had the appearance of being tenderly cared for, with each part carefully designed to encourage wildlife. It smelled of cut grass and of blossom hanging from the wild cherry tree. It had a fresh and exciting smell: every corner of the garden danced with life.

The garden was separated into three parts by bushes. It had a small flagstone path with steps linking them together. In the front part you could smell the nuts hanging from the bird feeders, and at the rear fresh mint from the side of the pond.

The garden grew progressively wilder further from the house. The first part, closest to the house, was mainly the patio and lawn, and had a bird bath that sparkled from the marbles in the water. In the centre it was like a small orchard – longer grass carpeted with wild flowers. The last section contained a garden shed, a natural small pond, a compost heap, and a wild meadow of undisturbed vegetation.

All year round, the garden felt like a secret paradise with a natural calm. It was pleasantly cool in summer from the

April's Pond

shade of the trees, and the bees came to collect pollen from the yellow lily flowers. In the winters, when hedgehogs hibernate, there was a time in the morning when everything glistened from early morning dew.

Mrs Robinson knew that the wild meadow next to the pond would make a good home for Milton. There he would be able to find snails, mushrooms, grass roots, worms, and an endless supply of small insects that hedgehogs love to eat.

Once a day, Hannah visited Milton at the bottom of the garden, and sometimes brought him some hedgehog mix or cat food. She was usually happy to just sit on the stone wall and watch Milton go about his business – burrowing his nose in the meadow for earthworms or finding a new place to take a nap.

Her visits were as much for her benefit as his. Whilst in the garden, she found it easy to relax and allow her imagination to roam around. Her thoughts always returned to the same thing. It was like an itch that needed to be scratched, and she had already made plans to scratch it.

One morning in July it was delightfully warm. Milton was napping at his favourite spot under the hedgerow next to the compost heap. He was only half asleep and stared at the white fluffy clouds. *I wonder what Hannah's doing*, he thought. *She hasn't been to see me in days.*

Just as he was about to doze off, something rustled in the bushes. Milton sat up straight, his eyes sprang open, and he stayed perfectly still. His eyes quickly searched back and forth in the bushes. He was sure something had moved. His heart began to race as he imagined a hungry fox looking for an easy meal. *I can't die like this!* He thought. *I haven't said goodbye to Hannah.*

A few minutes passed and there was no sign of the fox trying to sneak up on him. *Perhaps I imagined the whole thing,* he said to himself.

Just at that moment Milton saw something red and furry scurry out of the bushes and hide stealthily behind the shed. His heart was racing again, but faster. He quickly curled into a ball to protect his eyes from seeing the fox who was trying to eat him.

In truth he had never seen a fox, but his mother warned him of them at an early age … 'They were merciless creatures that could end a hedgehog's life in a blink of an eye, without hesitation and take you back to their young cubs for dinner.' He had often had nightmares about becoming a fox's lunch and now, perhaps, it was only moments from becoming a reality. 'Come out!' he shouted, from his ball. 'I'm not afraid of you.' But he was afraid, he was terrified.

After a full three minutes, Milton plucked up the courage to uncurl from his ball and take a peek. There was no sign of the fox. But standing there, right next to the pond, was a red-haired squirrel, who said, 'Quite strange… strange… yes, quite strange!'

The squirrel leant back and forth, and then stood on his hind legs. He was studying Milton and rapidly stroking his twitchy nose with his front legs.

'Was that *you* in the bushes?' asked Milton, still shaking. 'I thought you were a fox!'

'Quite interesting… interesting… yes, quite. You thought *I* was a fox, and *I* thought you were a rat carrying a bush. I couldn't imagine why a rat would be carrying a bush. So I just had to take a closer look.'

'You scared the life out of me running around in the bushes like that. I could have had a heart attack.'

He told the squirrel all about how he had escaped from certain death, thanks to Hannah, and ended up in the garden. The squirrel's name was Shaky due to his constant quivering, although he was merely remaining alert to danger. Shaky listened to Milton's story and seemed to be a good listener, but secretly he couldn't wait for him to finish his story.

'She's wonderful,' said Milton. 'I have never been as happy as when I am with her.'

'Girl you say? Never seen a *girl* here… not here…*no*, not here.'

'You don't suppose something has happened to her, do you? She hasn't been to visit for days.'

He looked around the garden and suddenly felt very cold and alone. It was like a warm comfy blanket had been snatched away from him. He paused, and then said, 'I have to find her!'

Shaky hopped closer to Milton and gave him a stern look. 'Milton, nothing good will come of this. But if you *must* find Hannah, you *might* try looking in the house at the bottom of the garden. That's where the humans live.'

Milton listened carefully as Shaky explained how to get there, which was quite difficult because the squirrel usually got there by leaping across the trees.

'Take care… yes, take care,' said Shaky, waving as he left.

Milton said goodbye to him and hurried down the garden path. There was no time to waste.

A few minutes later he stood at the entrance to the house. One of the patio doors had been left open and looked like an easy way inside.

'Be careful,' said a soft female voice.

He looked all around the entrance curiously, but could not see where the voice was coming from. After a few moments he wondered if the voice was inside his head – after all that *is* exactly what he was thinking.

'Over here, sitting on the little flower,' the quiet voice added.

He looked across the lawn and saw a little ladybird sitting on a daisy. It was no bigger than a peanut. It had a glorious, shiny red back and stunning black spots, which looked like beady eyes. The markings were clearly designed to ward off predators, but Milton thought she looked very innocent. The ladybird gave a flutter of its wings and flew a little closer to him. Landing on a dandelion, it spoke, 'My name is April, and it's a pleasure to meet you.'

'It's a pleasure to meet you too. I have to warn you though; I usually eat bugs like *you* for lunch.'

'Well,' she said. 'That would be *highly* undesirable for us both.'

April explained to Milton that ladybirds taste so awful that if anyone tried to eat her, they would quickly spit her out. She then rubbed her back legs together and made a little gooey liquid for Milton to taste.

He had no intention of eating her, but out of curiosity he couldn't resist a taste. He delicately stuck out his tongue and took a tiny amount of the sticky liquid from April's rear legs. At first it didn't taste too bad. Then as each second passed it grew more and more disgusting. A horrible burning sensation exploded on Milton's tongue, and it spread through his mouth like wildfire. He ran back and forth rolling into a ball, but it didn't help – it only got worse. It was like a volcano erupting, and felt lethal. 'Help, burning, burning!' he cried.

'Try to find some water;' she said, pointing and laughing. 'That puddle over there should help.'

Milton rolled across to the puddle and nearly drank the whole thing. As he drank, his thoughts once again returned to Hannah. He could spend hours making new friends and be no further in his mission. He must remain focused.

'Milton,' he said gasping for breath. 'My name is Milton. I'm trying to find a girl called Hannah. Can you help me? Is she in that house?'

'I'm not sure, I haven't been getting around that much lately. But I *do* know this. If you go to look for her in that house, you will be in *great* danger. It's not a safe place for creatures like us; you could easily be hurt or worse. A few of my friends have been killed in there.'

'I'm not afraid,' he lied, ruffling his spines. 'I have to find her, I miss her terribly and she might be in trouble.'

'I saw a mouse go in there a few weeks ago; he was flattened with a frying pan! Then there was the spider before that; he was stood on. Even the moth didn't make it; he was swatted with a newspaper. *So* enter at your peril, Milton!'

Milton stared at the open patio door once again. He had to find Hannah, no matter what the danger. He would have to be brave. There was a hole in his heart that only *she* could fill.

He remembered the first time she held him. When she looked into his eyes, her love bore into his heart – he felt safe – and it had remained there ever since.

'Good luck,' said April, as Milton began to creep through the door.

He had only just set foot in the house when Mr Robinson spotted him. He quickly scurried behind the couch they were sitting on for cover.

'By eck luv!' said Mr Robinson, jumping to his feet. 'Your hedge pig's in the house!' He was surprised and amused to see a hedgehog brave enough to come into the house. Normally wild animals avoid human contact. He guessed that this was due to Hannah's taking care of him recently; he had become domesticated and was now searching for someone to feed him.

'Get off my carpet!' cried Mrs Robinson.

The couple pulled back the couch; Milton was startled and quickly darted to the next chair to avoid them. All his senses were alive and sharp with the excitement, and he seemed to react instantly to the new danger. He thought about the warning that April had given, and then tried to put it out of his mind. Panicking would not help his situation.

'He's over 'ere Arthur,' she said pointing to the next chair. The couple moved towards it, one on either side.

A crowd of animals and insects gathered outside the patio window to watch Milton causing chaos in the Robinson's house.

'Run for the kitchen… run… yes, the kitchen,' shouted Shaky, excited.

'Don't give up!' said April.

'Leg it back this way!' tweeted one of the birds.

Milton was outnumbered and terrified. *I wish Hannah was here to save me!* He thought.

'Come on Milton!' said April, frustrated. 'Don't just stand there, *do* something!'

Milton dashed out from behind the chair and dodged left to avoid Mrs Robinson's hands. He ran as fast as he could back towards the patio door.

Mr Robinson got to the door seconds before Milton, and was about to close it when Milton gathered some momentum, tucked up into a ball, and rolled through Mr Robinson's legs just as the door slammed shut. Clunk!

Every creature in the garden breathed a sigh of relief. While watching Milton run around inside the house, they had each been willing him to survive and to succeed where others had failed. They wondered if they themselves would live through such an encounter.

It was such a close shave that Milton had lost one of his spines in the door. He paused to catch his breath. A feeling of complete failure ran through his tired muscles.

Just next to April, there was a house martin perched on the edge of the bird bath. It too had interrupted its usual chirrupy twitter to watch Milton's antics.

'That was impressive,' said Delia, the house martin.

'Looks like we have a very *special* hedgehog in our garden,' said April.

'If I was so *special* I would have found Hannah!' he replied.

'At least you're still alive Milton,' said Shaky. 'Not many could have escaped like that.'

'That's right,' said April, 'courage is a very admirable quality.'

He thanked the crowd for their support. He didn't feel very brave at all, quite the opposite in fact. He headed to the pond at the back of the garden to recover. He collapsed, exhausted, next to the compost heap to look at his front paws – they wouldn't stop shaking.

He spent the rest of the day waiting for Hannah in his usual spot under the hedgerow. He longed for her, but she never came.

Chapter 4 - Pond Life

The garden was a completely different place at night – the moonlight would play tricks with your mind, if you weren't careful. Dark shadows from the trees cast images of evil creatures that waited to jump out and surprise you. Ghosts would rustle the bushes and make the leaves swirl around on the patio. That evening was no exception; there was a smell in the air of rotten apples. It was as though a demon was at work and everything in the garden danced to the tune of his evil song.

Milton tried to keep his eyes closed and shuffled deeper into the hedgerow to feel safer. He couldn't sleep any longer though, and was starting to get a headache. He opened his eyes, stretched out his paws, and let out a yawn. It was only a few yards to the edge of the pond from where he slept. He walked over and swiped his paw into the cool water to splash his face; now he was awake. The first thought that came to his mind was also the last thought before he went to sleep, *where is Hannah?*

He could never imagine she would abandon him. That was ridiculous. *She will be along to see me soon*, he thought. He tried desperately to think of something special to do for her when she came.

April's Pond

A dark and creepy silhouette moved around in the pond, and for the first time Milton realized that the water was not empty. He was thirsty, but the thought of an underwater pond creature pulling him in while he took a drink was enough to quench his thirst.

Milton jumped with shock and nearly fell into the pond, as he felt something flutter behind his back.

'Good evening Milton,' said April. 'Can't you sleep? I didn't mean to surprise you. Ladybirds rarely surprise anyone.'

'I've been sleeping all day, actually. Hedgehogs are more awake at night.'

'Ah! So you're nocturnal, like an owl or a badger.'

Milton looked confused, 'Noc-what?'

'Nocturnal,' she repeated. 'It's just a fancy way of saying that you're a creature of the night.'

'That sounds clever, I'll remember that. What else do you know?'

'I know lots of things,' she said, proudly. 'Just recently I taught a spider how to climb.'

'That's not clever. I know *lots* of spiders that can climb.'

'Not *this* one, he was afraid of heights!'

Milton's eyes sprang open as a thought came to his mind. He stood silent for a moment to calculate his plan and then burst into action, 'You just gave me a fantastic idea! I'll be back in a minute.' Then he ran off behind the shed in a hurry.

There was a loud clang of metal, which indicated that Milton had knocked down the garden spade leaning on the shed.

'You woke me up!' shouted a voice in the tree. It was Shaky. 'Haven't you any idea what time it is? *You* may stay awake all night but squirrels certainly do not!'

'Sorry,' he said, looking up. 'But now that you're awake, could you lend me a hand?'

'Help you? It's the middle of the night! What on earth are you up to?'

Shaky ran down the tree. He moved at great speed for someone who had just woken up. He examined an old wooden crate that Milton was attempting to drag back towards the pond. He would never be able to move it alone. He was still not quite awake or sure of what was going on, but he decided to help him anyway.

'On the count of three, lift!' said Milton. Struggling with the weight, they both lifted the crate and, after a few steps, took a rest until the box was in the middle of the meadow. The pair tilted the box onto its end, and made it stand upright. It was nearly three times their height.

'This *better* be worth it,' said the Shaky. 'Mad… Quite mad… yes, quite mad.'

'I'm not mad. Hannah will be coming to visit me soon, and I want to impress her.'

'I don't think she will be very impressed by a dusty old crate,' said April, with a giggle.

'April, can you teach me to climb up that crate like the spider, and do something impressive for Hannah?'

She thought for a moment, and then said, 'I'll certainly try. I am a very talented coach after all, and modest too. You're not afraid of heights, are you?'

'No,' he lied.

'Good. How about a back flip from the top then?'

Milton gazed up at the peak of the crate and imagined himself perched on the cliff's edge at Parker's Abbey. He looked down at the water and experienced a sinking feeling in his stomach. He tried to calm himself by breathing deeply a few times, but it was no good. As he walked to the bottom of the crate his right paw began to shake.

'Are you *sure* you're alright, Milton?' asked April.

'I just don't want to hurt myself, that's all. It's a long way up if I don't make it.'

'You could put it next to the pond,' suggested Shaky. 'That wouldn't hurt so much then, if you make a mistake... no, not much... quite safe in fact.'

Milton's thoughts again returned to Parker's Abbey. Hannah was very impressed when Adam leaped from the top. Surely this would have the same effect.

'Okay,' he said. 'I'll do it. But perhaps we should leave it until the morning when the water is a little warmer.'

'That sounds like a good plan. You will feel *much* fresher then. Let's all meet back here in the morning.'

As everyone said goodnight and April flew off, Milton nudged the crate closer to the pond and stared at the top. *What have I agreed to?* He thought.

In the morning, the whole garden came back to life – the birds were awake and singing in concert, the sun's warmth had lit up the pond and reflected the image of a magnificent oak tree, and the meadow smelled of roses. It was as if an angel had swept her arm across the garden and made everything shine.

A curious crowd of animals and insects gathered around the wooden crate next to the pond. There were stag beetles perched on an old tree trunk, blue tits hopping between branches in the hedgerow, and bumble bees buzzing past everyone. Shaky and April had a front-row seat and had positioned themselves on the edge of an upturned plant pot.

'I'm not too late, am I April?' asked Delia from the air. She fluttered her wings and landed on top of the crate to join them. House martins are renowned for being late, and Delia was no exception.

'No, you're just in time. Here he comes now.'

Milton walked out from the hedgerow, rubbed his eyes, and looked around at the crowd in disbelief. Everyone he had met in the last few days had come to see *him* perform. As he stretched out his arms and took a deep breath, he said, 'No pressure then!'

'Okay Milton,' said April, in a firm voice. 'Let's take this one step at a time. First you need to warm up your muscles and have a good stretch!'

He did exactly as he was told. First he moved his head from side to side, then circled his arms backwards and forwards, and after that he began to jog around the outside of the pond.

'That's good, Milton. A little faster now and lift up your knees.'

After a few minutes when Milton's breathing was like a steam train, and the colour of his cheeks turned pink. He said, 'I'm not sure I can do much more of this!'

'Okay, Milton, that's enough. Hold it there and have a good stretch.'

At some point during the warm up he had forgotten about the height of the box and the acrobatics he was expected to perform. Now, however, it all came flooding back. Something deep inside his brain was screaming at him not to take risks. But he had to take a risk. How else could he ever win Hannah's affections? What kind of a hedgehog would he become, if he always chose the path of the least danger? Certainly not the kind that Hannah would admire!

The crowd began to push each other for a better view of the spectacle.

'Right, what next?' asked Milton hesitantly.

'Now stand at the bottom of crate, and climb up to the top. Remember to keep a firm grip on the wooden planks, and don't look down.'

That's easy for you to say, thought Milton. He pulled on the first plank, which felt very loose, and pulled himself up. Just before the top of the crate, his leg began to shake uncontrollably from balancing on his toes; his right foot slipped off the plank. He panicked, tightened his grip with his hands, and held himself steady.

'Are you alright, Milton?' shouted Shaky.

'You can do it!' said Delia, fluttering her wings. 'Keep going.'

Milton put his forehead onto the crate and took a deep breath. *Please let me get through this*, he said to himself. A moment later, he gathered the courage to keep climbing. Taking one step at a time, he made steady progress, until eventually he clambered over the top lip of the crate, slowly stood upright, and breathed a sigh of relief.

'Well done Milton!' complimented Shaky. '*Well* done indeed.'

'Yes, good work,' said April. 'Now, for the tricky part; I want you to stand at the edge of the crate with your back to the water and balance on your toes.'

I can do this, he thought, nervously. *I can't back out now.*

As he shuffled to the edge, his stomach started churning and made him feel sick. He looked down and saw the fishes swim around at the back of the pond and then felt dizzy too. *Try to relax*, he thought to himself.

As he turned to put his back to the pond, a light breeze made the balancing awkward.

April shuffled forward on the plant pot to get a better view and then said, 'Excellent! Now stand with your feet and knees together and your arms by your sides. Then, when I say go, I want you to bend your knees and try to throw your arms and legs back over your head.'

Milton stood in the correct position and closed his eyes. For a moment he couldn't hear anything around him. The noise of the crowd was gone. He imagined himself leaping off the top of the crate and making the perfect dive into the pond. In his mind he saw Hannah's face watching him. It brought a warm and calm feeling into his heart. He smiled and opened his eyes; he was ready now. This was for Hannah.

The crate wobbled as Milton launched from the top. There was complete silence as he flipped over backwards through the air. Most of the crowd held their breath and then let out a sigh of relief as he landed feet first into the water. Splash!

Everyone in the crowd was cheering as he emerged from the water. He had an enormous grin across his face. 'I'm doing that again!' he said, dripping wet. 'It was much easier than I thought it would be!'

Milton climbed back up the crate, twice as fast as before.

Before jumping he winked down at April, and she smiled proudly back up at him. 'Geronimo!'

The shade of grass tussocks and woven branches at the edge of the garden made an excellent camouflage. Tabatha had been watching the pond's antics all morning from the gaps in the branches, and no one could see her. Her black silky coat blended into the shadows perfectly. If anyone had stumbled across her hideout they would have been in for a deadly surprise.

From where she was curled up, it was easy to see the crowd next to the pond – all watching Milton performing his tricks. She licked her razor-sharp claws and stared at Milton. Her marble green eyes were fixated on his figure. She imagined pouncing on him from a dark corner and pinning him to the floor with her claws. Her strong jaws and teeth would be more than a match for him. She shook with hatred for the little hedgehog. It would be easy to kill him – not just because he was innocent of how cruel the world can be, but because she knew she could kill him without feeling a moment of guilt. She hadn't always been like that. *Life* had made her that way.

Enjoy your life while you still have one, Milton, she thought.

Chapter 5 - Lost and Found

The garden had some excellent hiding places. You could hide behind the shed, the flower pots, in the bushes, behind the tree trunks, and underneath garden tools. In the long grass and the hedgerow, there was an unlimited supply of dark corners to squeeze into. Some of the plants and flowers were even better. If you stayed perfectly still, it was nearly impossible to see you from a distance.

Milton and April were playing a game of hide-and-seek, and they had been playing for hours. First April hid and Milton counted to one hundred, before he went to look for her. She was much better at hiding than him because she was so much smaller. Once she had disappeared for nearly twenty minutes.

Milton finished counting and began to search for her. After ten minutes, he had searched everywhere in the garden. He'd looked at all the usual places – the garden pots, behind the shed, and even inside a daffodil flower. Eventually, he found her in the rough patch at the very back of the garden. She was sitting on a broad dock leaf, fighting with another insect.

'Are you alright, April? Do you need some help?'

She was holding a green fly in her mouth. It was shaking its legs as fast as it could, but looked completely helpless. After a few seconds the legs stopped moving and April put it down on the leaf.

'Absolutely fine! I'm just about to have this little aphid for lunch. Would you like to join me?'

April's Pond

Milton looked at the little greenfly that she had bitten in half and screwed up his face. He didn't imagine her being capable of something like that. He had only known April for a short time, but she always appeared so gentle and caring. He told himself that she had to live somehow, just like he did. After all, he didn't consider *himself* to be cruel, even though he ate live insects of *all* shapes and sizes.

'Doesn't he look appetizing?' asked April, delighted. 'All that green goo!'

'I don't think I have ever eaten a *green* insect before. And I don't intend to start now; you're quite welcome to him.'

After lunch the pair went to the patio to sit in the sun for a while.

Delia was busy collecting food from one of the hanging bird feeders and twittering a song to herself. 'There you are,' she said, flying over. She looked very excited and said, 'I've been looking everywhere for you two. Anyone would think you were hiding. I have some great news!'

'Okay, spit it out then,' said April.

Delia flew closer to make sure they heard her properly. Folks often had trouble hearing what she said. She put her black bill in the air and proudly showed her white bellied under parts.

'Come on then,' said Milton. 'What is it?'

Delia would not be rushed, and loved to be the centre of attention. She did an excellent imitation of a world leader making a speech and said, 'I, Delia Feathernest, have found the young girl you have been missing. I was flying back from the lake, after a successful hunting trip, when just a few streets away I saw a family with two children entering a house. I flew closer and overheard the oldest man refer to the young girl as Hannah!'

'That's wonderful!' said Milton, beaming. 'Can you give me the directions?'

'I knew you would be pleased,' she sang.

The House Martin explained where Hannah was, but it was complicated and difficult to understand. Milton had never flown in the air before, and couldn't imagine the route she was describing.

'Thank you, Delia,' he said. 'I'm still not sure how to get there, but I have to try and find it.'

April and Delia watched him make his preparations for the journey. He took a drink from the pond, dug up a worm, and practiced rolling into a ball. That way he would not be thirsty or hungry, and if anything nasty came along he would be ready for it.

'Goodbye Milton,' said April. 'See you soon.'

'Yes, take care,' said Delia. 'And be careful.'

He went to the back of the garden just like Delia had described. He pushed his way through the thick brambles, scratching his belly, and emerged onto Smuggler's Lane.

The tree house in the Del was empty during the day, when the children were at school. It had been built solidly by the local children with a little help from concerned parents. From its roof you could see above all the houses in every direction.

It was the perfect lookout for Tabatha. From here she studied each house and garden, and absorbed everything she saw. If carefully planned, a free meal could be stolen from an unsuspecting housewife's kitchen, without being detected. But much better than this was the prospect of a meal you earned, a hunted meal.

She sat on the roof and looked down Smuggler's Lane with her keen and sharp eyes. There was a subtle movement in the leaves outside the Robinson's house, that most would miss, but Tabatha saw it. It betrayed Milton's location. Her eyes widened, when she realized it was him. She watched the spiky brown hedgehog pop his head out and look around. Her muscles tensed and she dug her claws into the roof. She imagined the hedgehog was in her reach and that the roof was his body. As she scratched at the roof it released some of the anger she felt. Her plan was clear. *I could set up an ambush*, she thought. *I could wait patiently in the Lane behind a fence post, and then spring my trap. He wouldn't know what hit him.*

She continued to study him as he got further up the woodland alley. Just above him flew the House Martin, keeping an eye on his progress. *I can't allow a witness*, thought Tabatha. *I must make sure he's alone when I kill him. It must be when he least expects it.*

After thirty minutes of walking, Milton sat on his back paws and took a few deep breaths. Overhead he could see Delia circling and trying to shout directions. He tried to listen but couldn't hear a thing because of the wind whistling down the Lane. *Thanks for trying*, he thought.

As he walked down the lane, he could smell the most unusual thing. He concentrated on the smell and tried hard to remember what it reminded him of. It brought back memories of playing on the kitchen floor with Hannah… happy memories.

'Lamb joint!' he said, exited, and thought, *All I have to do is follow the smell and I'll be back in Mrs Watt's kitchen.*

He pitched his nose into the air and began to zigzag down Smuggler's Lane, following the smell with his nose. When the smell was stronger he kept going in that direction. Eventually he saw something that made him smile. He looked up into the kitchen window of a house and saw Mrs Watt washing the dishes. Milton was overwhelmed with emotion. He had finally found what he was looking for. His bottom lip began to quiver, and he tried to hold back the tears of joy. Then he stopped trying.

'Hannah,' called Mrs. Watt, impatiently. 'Have you finished unpacking yet? Dinner's nearly ready.'

'Not yet, Mum,' she replied. 'Where do you want me to put the sun tan lotion?'

Sun tan lotion? Unpacking? thought Milton. *Of course! They must have been on a holiday. That's why Hannah hasn't been to see me. I knew there would be a good explanation!*

He was curious to see what was happening inside the house. In the backyard, there was a newly cut plank of wood leaning next to the kitchen window. It was surrounded by woodwork tools. He avoided the sharp tools and climbed up the plank; from there he could see everything that was going on inside the house. Mrs Watt was putting away some shopping into the fridge, Mr Watt was searching through his toolbox, and Hannah was tugging at her mothers dress.

'Can I go out after dinner, Mum?' asked Hannah.

'Are you going to see your little friend again?' she replied.

'Yes! I really missed him while I was away. I've got something special for him too.'

'Well, alright then. But don't be late back home.'

Great! thought Milton. *I'd better get back and practice my trick to impress her.*

Without a second thought, Milton ran down the plank and out of the backyard. He didn't want to waste any time. Hannah was much faster than him, so he would have to hurry.

It took only fifteen minutes to get back to the Robinson's garden. As fast as he could, he did a back flip from the top of the crate into the pond to make sure he could do it right and then waited for Hannah to arrive.

April, Shaky, and Delia all came to the pond to watch his happy moment.

'I'm so proud of you,' said April. 'That little girl is very lucky to have a special hedgehog like you.'

'Very lucky,' said Shaky. 'Yes, lucky… very lucky, indeed.'

Milton waited patiently as the time passed, and it grew darker. April, Shaky, and Delia kept him company but, after a while, they feared he would be disappointed. They just didn't want to hurt his feelings by telling him.

Another hour passed, the sky turned grey, a cold breeze came into the garden, and it began to rain.

'I'm sorry Milton,' said April. 'I don't think she's coming.'

'She's coming,' he said stubbornly. 'I heard her say it! She wouldn't let me down. Something must have happened.'

'Come on,' said Delia, to the others. 'Let's leave him alone for a while.'

As the three of them left, he turned to face the pond. That way they wouldn't see him get upset. He waited there all evening and long into the night but, once again, she never came.

Chapter 6 - Practice Makes Permanent

Squirrels are clever and persistent animals. In the Watt's and the neighbour's gardens, they were notorious for eating out of the bird feeders, digging in potted plants – either to bury or recover seeds – and for setting up house in sheltered areas, including attics. Shaky was a typical squirrel.

Many of the local companies sold bird feeders which are supposedly 'squirrel-proof,' very few of them really are. Early spring was the hardest time of the year for Shaky and the other squirrels, this is when buried nuts begin to sprout and new ones don't exist. Shaky preferred to find his own nuts and leave the feeders for Delia; but at this time of the year he had no choice.

The best time to steal nuts was early in the morning, at first light. This was when Mr Robinson and his wife were asleep. They would just presume the birds had taken them.

Milton sat nearby with April and watched the squirrel scamper up the cherry blossom tree. He balanced on the bottom branch and then hung upside down.

'That looks very dangerous,' said Milton. 'Aren't you afraid?'

'No. Not at all,' said Shaky. 'I rely on my skill, and I practice a lot!'

They smiled with fascination at Shaky's gymnastic ability. It was no wonder April called him a tree rat. The look of concentration in his eyes was intense. He was focused on the hanging feeder swinging on a thread a few feet below the branch. If he missed, the result would be a catastrophe.

The wind picked up and Milton watched through his paws, afraid to see what might happen if he fell.

Shaky leapt from the branch and caught the feeder easily. For a moment it looked like he could fly. 'Ta-dah!' he said, triumphantly. He was clearly pleased with his own performance.

'That was amazing,' said Milton. 'How long did it take you to learn that?'

'Well,' said Shaky. 'At first I wasn't that good. But I stuck at it; I practiced every day, and, after a while, I was an expert. I find that if you try hard enough, and long enough, you eventually get what you want.'

'There's a lesson to be learned there, Milton,' said April.

'You're right. I'm not giving up on Hannah! I have to see her and show her what she is missing.'

April said goodbye and watched her obsessed friend scurry off towards Smuggler's Lane.

Milton pushed through the bushy entrance to the woodland alley and sat still for a moment. He put his head into his paws, squeezed his eyes tight, and concentrated hard to remember the route. After a few seconds, he opened his eyes. He had the feeling he was being watched, but dismissed it, and started walking the route with a spring in his step.

After twenty minutes, he heard Hannah's familiar voice.

'Stop it!' she said, giggling. 'It tickles!'

A smile of joy came to Milton's face when he heard Hannah laughing from inside the house. He knew instantly she was alright. He felt relieved. It was like the rain had stopped, and the dark clouds were replaced by bright sunshine and a magnificent rainbow.

His eyes darted back and forth desperately. He was looking for the plank of wood that led conveniently to the kitchen window, but it was gone. He quickly followed the outside of the building to the side of the house. From there he spotted the large glass double doors of the living room and hurried to see Hannah's face inside.

When he looked into the room, he froze like a statue. His eyes were wide open and his jaw dropped. It was like his heart had fallen from his chest, the life squeezed out.

'Would you like to listen to some music?' asked Hannah, from inside the house. 'What's your favourite band?'

'Yeah,' said Adam. 'That would be great. You choose something.'

Hannah sprang up from the couch, collected a few discs, and leapt back into the seat next to him. Adam looked through her collection of music. After studying a couple of tracks he looked up to smile at Hannah. She was playing with her hair and beaming back at him.

'Seen anything you like?' asked Hannah, blushing.

'I see you!'

The pair stopped smiling and stared into each others eyes. Hannah brushed the hair from her face in anticipation. Adam leaned forward, paused for a moment, and then kissed her lips.

Oh no! thought Milton, devastated. *How could I have been so stupid? She didn't miss me at all. She's probably forgotten all about me!*

He couldn't help watching the couple through the glass doors even though the pain was uncontrollable. He dropped his forehead onto the glass door in desperation. Tears streamed down his face, he was sobbing and shaking uncontrollably. It felt like the world had been designed just to torture him. He continued to watch and hoped that somehow it was just his imagination; but it wasn't.

It began to rain – slow at first, then a heavy downpour. It was like Mother Nature herself was sharing his pain. The rain was cold, but he didn't care about that anymore. *I wish I were dead!* He sobbed.

Mrs Watt's car on the driveway hardly ever moved. The sticker on the bumper read: 'I brake for scholar's priests and no apparent reason'. Underneath the car was a clear view to the side of the house, and it provided an excellent cover from the rain.

Tabatha arched her back underneath the car and rubbed herself against the inside of the tyres, to satisfy an itch.

Another itch will soon be satisfied, she thought. No one ever looked underneath the car and would never suspect she was there. She stretched out her paws and rolled across her back gracefully.

So, the little hedgehog wants to die. You won't be disappointed, Milton, I promise. But I think you should suffer a little first. So the inevitable can wait.

She watched with an evil grin as he hobbled back to the Robinson's garden. He looked heart broken; she was pleased to see that.

Chapter 7 - A Nice Surprise

Spring was well and truly over. The sun was rising earlier every day and the heat, at times, was unbearable. The lawn had grown to almost a foot in length, and it desperately needed cutting. The garden looked very different. Flowers that were previously hidden below the ground were springing up all over; they had opened their petals, which added wonderful red and yellow colours to the normal green view. Golden dandelions were everywhere, and the bottom of the garden in the meadow was no different.

Most of the creatures in the garden were relaxing or going about their business lazily. The warm weather seemed to drain the energy off everyone, except the greenfly and aphids who buzzed around everyone's noses to annoy them. Milton sat at the edge of the lawn and swung his paws angrily at a cloud of them. His soul felt bruised, and the little flies added to the torment.

'Are you alright Milton?' asked April, from the flower bed.

'They're doing it on purpose! I think they've told their friends to tease me just for fun.'

'Don't be silly. Aphids *can't* think or talk. Besides which, they'll all be gone soon.'

'Oh really, why is that? Surely you can't eat them all.'

'I'll have a little help. I'm going to give birth soon, and ladybird babies are hungry little critters. We ladybirds eat thousands of aphids in just one year.'

Milton's face instantly lit up when he realized what he had just heard.

'Did you just say that you were going to have babies!' he shrieked. 'That's wonderful. Congratulations! Are you hoping for a boy or a girl?'

'Well, I imagine there will be quite a few of each. I'll be laying about 1,500 eggs!'

'I'm going to be an uncle,' he said, proudly. 'I'll be an uncle to thousands of cute little ladybirds. I can't wait!'

'Somehow, I don't think you will have to wait long,' she said. 'I feel almost ready. I just need to find somewhere suitable to lay my eggs.'

Milton began to jump around with excitement. He dashed around the garden gathering Delia and Shaky together.

'April's going to have babies,' he announced. 'Thousands of them, and I'll be an Uncle!'

April fiddled with her wings and looked uncomfortable with being the centre of attention.

'That's fantastic,' said Shaky. 'We could do with a bit of life around here.'

April explained what was required for a suitable nest. Everyone was deep in thought, and looked puzzled. They couldn't think of anything like April described.

'Right,' said Delia, finally. 'We can't sit around all day. Let's split up to find a suitable place for April's eggs. She can't wonder around all over the place in her present condition.'

Delia pointed with her wings, as if conducting an orchestra, and gave everyone an area to search. Shaky hopped around at the front of the garden, Milton the rear, and Delia flew up and down Smuggler's Lane.

After a few minutes of searching behind the old shed, Milton's nose began to twitch, he smelled something unusual.

He had been trained to search out mysterious smells from an early age. His father had invented a game to improve this skill that would result in a delicious treat if he won. Now each time he searched for the source of a smell, he was reminded of the fun he used to have with his father, which made him smile.

He dug around in the hedgerow and pricked his paw on something sharp. He blinked a couple of times and rubbed his eyes to make sure he wasn't mistaken. Underneath a couple of weeds was a short brown spine with a black tip. *This is not mine*, he thought.

A shiver went up his back, like he was being watched. He screwed up his face and looked around for the intruder, but he couldn't see anyone.

Typical, he thought. *Now there's another hedgehog to steal all my food; as if I don't have enough problems!*

When he returned to the pond he saw April sitting on Delia's back and smiling.

'Did you find anything?' asked Milton.

'It was *I* that found it,' said Delia. 'And it wasn't easy you know. It's very dangerous for a house martin to go wondering around on the floor. I might get eaten by a fox, or worse!'

She described the place to the others that was to become home for April's babies. 'It's not far away; just down the lane, in fact. There's a little spot in between some houses with an old tree trunk. It's packed full of aphids and should be perfect.'

Delia was describing the Del. Milton shuddered, he remembered the close encounter he had there with the hangman's noose. 'Be careful, April,' he warned. 'Is there anything you want me to do?'

'No thanks, I'll be fine. Don't worry about me. I'll be back soon.'

Milton and Shaky waved goodbye, as Delia flew off with April hitching a lift on her back.

'Shaky,' said Milton. 'I think there is another hedgehog around here stealing my food. If you spot him, can you help me scare him off?'

Shaky made fists with his paws and showed his teeth. 'No problem,' he said, menacingly. 'I can be terrifying when I want to be, you know.'

The Del was shaded by the surrounding trees and was considerably cooler than the Robinson's garden. Tabatha walked slowly and carefully through the bushes – she was like a jungle soldier on patrol. She stopped suddenly and looked surprised. *You don't see that everyday*, she thought. *A ladybird flying on a house martin's back!*

She sat patiently and watched them land next to an old log. It took nearly an hour, but eventually, Delia flew away. She crept towards the old log and peered inside from a distance, so she couldn't be seen. Next to the ladybird were hundreds of shiny little yellow eggs. She watched for the next two hours as April laid hundreds more.

Chapter 8 - Let the Show Begin!

The most exciting event of the morning was Mr Robinson cutting the lawn. Almost three days had passed since April left the garden, but it felt like a month. Milton looked around the garden and saw everyone was busy, except him. Delia was perched on the roof of the house and singing away with some younger birds. It looked like she was at an important meeting and was having an argument with one of the swallows.

Shaky sat on his favourite tree satisfying his addiction – frantically eating some discarded chewing gum. He became a different person when he was chewing – short-tempered, aggressive, and even paranoid.

Milton was afraid to disturb him; he had his own chewing habit and started chomping on a grass root. *I'm bored*, he thought.

The patio doors opened and Hannah emerged from the house. She began searching around in one of the bushes then looked across the lawn and smiled.

'Milton!' she shouted. 'There you are.'

Her voice shuddered through his body and he went numb; his eyes opened wide and his body froze solid. He was caught off guard. *That's Hannah's voice*, he thought. *Now's my chance!*

He burst into life and ran for the pond. When he reached the back of the garden his legs hurt from the sprint, and he could hardly breathe. He started to climb the crate and a breeze shook it. His body tensed up, and it didn't feel right: a look of fear came across his face and he squeezed his eyes shut.

You can do this, he thought to himself. *I'm jumping from this crate, even if it kills me.*

Hannah skipped over to the pond, still grinning, and watched him perching on the edge of the crate. 'Where did you go?' she asked, confused.

He stood proudly, like a world champion gymnast ready to perform. Then he put his feet and knees together, dropped his hands to his sides, and confidently threw his legs over his head and into the pond. Splash!

Hannah threw her arms into the air, clapped her hands, and jumped up and down uncontrollably. She was so surprised that she nearly lost her balance and fell into the pond herself.

'Ha ha!' she laughed. 'Super! Where on earth did you learn to do that?'

He kicked his legs, swam to the side, and pulled himself out of the pond.

'And you can swim too,' said Hannah, amazed. 'Come here.'

She scooped him up and danced back to the patio with him in her arms.

That should do it, thought Milton, beaming. *She will forget all about that boy now, since she's seen how special I am.*

The hours seemed to pass in minutes for Milton. Hannah played his favourite game of fetch, and he made the most of every second. He ran as fast as possible and occasionally rolled into a ball, which always made her laugh. 'Well done,' she said. 'You're getting so fast!'

He felt like the first hedgehog on the moon. Hannah's smiling eyes cut right through his soul, and warmed him like campfire. He felt as if his purpose on earth was to make her happy.

Soon the sun had dropped below the houses, and Hannah looked at her watch.

Don't go! he thought.

'I have to go,' she said. 'But I'll come back and see you soon, and I'll bring a surprise for you.'

He watched her leaving through the patio windows. She said goodbye to Mr and Mrs Robinson and then left without even looking back at the garden.

The kitchen was busier than ever when Hannah arrived home. Mr Watt was helping Robert with his homework at the table, and Mrs Watt was rolling pastry on the worktop.

'What have you been up to, Hannah?' asked Mrs Watt.

'I went to see Milton,' she said. 'He's incredibly clever, you know. He did a back flip and he can even swim.'

'You should enter him in the school talent contest,' said Robert. 'I'm going to be a magician. I have a wand and everything.'

'Yeah,' said Mr Watt. 'That would be a first. He could be famous.'

'Don't be silly,' said Hannah. 'The whole school will be there. Everyone knows that it's just for kids. Besides which, I don't really have time for Milton anymore.'

Tabatha was lying in her bed. She stretched out her legs and twitched uncontrollably. She was having a nightmare. It always began the same, with the boy's face: he was *delighted*. She was terrified, and then came the skin-tearing pain.

Robert had made a whip. It was crudely manufactured from a broken broomstick handle with several cut lengths of string. He had tied the string to the handle and knotted the string, because that would hurt more.

Each time the whip cracked, she braced herself for immense pain that followed.

The living room doors were closed and there was nowhere to run, but she ran anyway to spare herself the unbearable pain for a few more seconds.

She ran, and he laughed. The whip cracked and tore her skin. He laughed again.

When she eventually woke up, she studied the scars on her legs and back, and then licked them; perhaps it would help to soothe the memories.

Chapter 9 – Encore

It was late in the evening and the garden was pleasantly quiet. Most of the garden's creatures had settled down for the evening, and the sun was hidden behind the hedge.

Milton, however, was wide awake and taking a dip in the pond. He was singing cheerfully, 'There's a bright golden haze on the meadoooooow! There's a bright golden haze on the meadowwwwwww!!'

Shaky heard the commotion and scampered across the lawn to see what was going on. He was naturally inquisitive, like most squirrels, and hated to miss out on any action. When he arrived, he was out of breath. 'What are you so happy about?'

'Just happy to be alive,' said Milton. 'I spent a wonderful day with Hannah and life is just great!'

'One minute you're down, the next you're up! I can't keep up with you.'

Shaky watched, highly amused, while Milton whistled a tune and swam around in the pond.

'Have you heard any news about April?' asked Milton.

'I did see her earlier; I think she must be missing you. She was constantly asking about you. Perhaps you'd better go and see her.'

'You're right; I'd better go over there. With everything happening today, I'd forgotten all about her.'

He swam to the edge, jumped out and shook himself dry. After a few minutes he was ready to visit his friend.

He felt guilty for letting April slip from his mind. He didn't like to be selfish, but he felt that, occasionally, it was okay to put his own happiness first. After all, she was in no danger.

When he got to the Del, April spotted him immediately and fluttered over to greet him. The Del seemed a lot friendlier than his last visit, even though the sun was almost gone. 'Hello, stranger! What brings you to this neck of the woods?'

He smiled, and detected a note of disappointment in April's voice. 'How are you? How are my new nephews and nieces?' he asked, looking around.

'Oh, don't worry about them. They're going to be just fine. Tell me all about your visit from Hannah.'

'I see you have been talking to Delia! It was wonderful, thanks to you. I showed her the trick you taught me, and she was extremely impressed. I've never been so happy.'

'Excellent,' she said. 'What are you planning to do next?'

'Next? I haven't thought about that.'

'Well, you'd better do something. You don't want her to lose interest, do you?'

He frowned and searched for an answer. It hadn't occurred to him until now that he would have to perform new tricks on a regular basis. Was it even possible to continually come up with a new act? He would definitely need help, if he was going to try and keep her interested. 'Can you teach me something new, April?'

'I thought you'd never ask. I have just the thing! Come over here.'

April led the way to some clear ground next to a large oak tree and an old rotting log.

'Right,' she said. 'You already know how to do a back flip; now I want you to do it without the box and on the ground. It's more difficult, but technically the same and a lot more impressive.'

'That *does* sound difficult. But I'll give it a try, April.'

'First, try it from the top of the log. Then, when you're up to it, give it a go on the ground.'

He climbed up the small log and stood at the end, while April gathered some leaves and heather at the bottom of the log to cushion the landing. It didn't seem as scary as the crate, but a mistake would be much worse.

'Okay, Milton. Concentrate now, and keep your legs together.'

He counted to three, then confidently leapt from the log, and easily landed on his feet with only a slight stumble. 'That was much easier than I thought it would be!'

'You're a natural,' she said. 'You've come a long way from the hedgehog I first met. A few more goes, get your legs a little higher each time and then you will be ready to try it on the ground.'

After just half an hour's practice, he was proficient. He could back flip easily from the log and on the ground.

'Okay, you're ready! You must show Hannah your new skill immediately, while it's fresh in your mind.'

Ladybirds are often impatient, but April's enthusiasm was overwhelming.

'What... now?'

'Delia flew over this afternoon. She told me that Hannah's family is having a party in the garden. Hannah *should* be back there by now. This is the perfect opportunity for you to impress her in front of everyone.'

'Perfect!' he said. 'Thank you, April; you really are wonderful. You're a true friend.'

Milton headed for Smugglers Lane. 'Take care of those babies!'

April watched him leave, and wiped a tear from her eye. 'Goodbye Milton.'

Chapter 10 - A Party to Remember

When Milton arrived at Hannah's backyard, it was very late. The moon was hidden behind a cloud and without its light, he kept bumping into the garden furniture that had been left out. There was no sign of life anywhere – even the house lights had been switched off. He suddenly felt lonely, but not alone. 'Looks like I missed the party.'

'Oh no, Milton, the party is about to begin!' said a voice from behind him.

He jumped with fright. His spines pricked up all over his back; a cold shiver ran down his spine. He squinted his eyes and stared into the blackness.

'Who's there?' he asked, timidly. 'Come out!'

His eyes began to get used to the darkness, and he could make out the shape of an animal much taller and bigger than him. Its ears were pointed and pricked up like knife blades; it had golden glowing eyes and whiskers that shined silver. This was no fox; it was too small, but it looked even more terrifying and predatory.

'Remember *me*, Milton?' said Tabatha. 'Remember living in *my* house and eating *my* food?'

'T…Tabby?' he said, stuttering. 'Tabby cat is that you? You had me scared there for a moment.'

She crept closer to Milton, within striking distance. Her tail was balanced straight above her back and it moved majestically towards him with each of her strides. Swinging her tail helped her to think – to calculate her enemies' moves before they made them. A twitch of a shoulder, a deep breath, even a wink of an eye would be enough to give her an advantage.

'I should be very scared if I were you, Milton. Your days of entertaining Hannah and your friends at the pond are over. You can leave that to me now. You see, that food you stole so happily wasn't free and, now, you are going to pay for it… with your life!'

'Wait,' he said. 'Don't do this! Can't we be friends? I don't deserve to be killed, do I?'

'You *are* truly pathetic, Milton. I might have known you would beg for your life.'

Tabatha's mouth opened into an evil grin which showed off her fanged teeth and snake-like tongue. 'Hannah is going to find your miserable body lying on the kitchen floor tomorrow morning. She'll probably just bury you in the garden, visit her boyfriend, and forget all about you.'

She wouldn't get over him just like that. Milton imagined Hannah kneeling down, and crying over his body. She would be consoled by her mother, who, no doubt, would see it as a great learning experience to develop her daughter emotionally. He couldn't let it happen, not without putting up a fight.

'Do your worst, you stupid cat!' he said angrily.

Tabatha's tail began to swish back and forth faster than before – it was distracting. She watched and waited for her opportunity to strike. In a heart beat, she swung her paw full of sharp claws at Milton's head. He ducked, and pricked up his spines. She hit them, cried out, and jumped backwards. She struck again, with her teeth. She bit his feet. He reacted instantly by curling into a ball. He pricked her again, *hard*. She shrieked with pain and rolled away, hurt. A light came on in the house from the bathroom and blinded Tabatha. It was just the opportunity Milton needed. He wasted no time and rolled forward again. This time *he* grabbed *Tabatha's* leg and bit her as hard as he could. She screamed and shook her leg to free it. She was hurt and bleeding too.

Tabatha was unprepared for this. No one *ever* stood up to her. This wasn't supposed to be a *real* fight. It wasn't meant to be a struggle at all. Milton seemed not a mere hedgehog at all, but strong and invincible. She needed to escape in order to lick her wounds, so she ran limping out of the yard to the street at the front of the house and took cover under the car.

'And don't come back!' he shouted, proudly.

It was over as quickly as it started. The fight had lasted for just a few seconds, but somehow he was exhausted and drained.

The walk back to the pond seemed endless. Every muscle in Milton's body seemed to ache. His right paw was bleeding and the left felt broken – the pain was almost unbearable. He hadn't noticed the injury until a few minutes after the fight, when his heart had stopped racing, but now it was intense.

He walked for what seemed forever. Eventually the pain was too much, and he felt incredibly tired. His eyes rolled around and he felt dizzy. There was a ringing sound in his ears, and then he stumbled and collapsed at the side of Smuggler's Lane.

Chapter 12 - The Revelation

The next morning in the garden started with a bang. Shaky sprinted across the lawn to the cherry blossom tree where Delia was sitting; she was studying the shortage of nuts in the bird feeder.

'Delia, come quick!' said Shaky. 'Milton's lying in the lane and I think he's hurt!'

'Are you sure?' she replied. 'He does sleep in some strange places.'

'Yes, but he isn't usually covered in blood!'

'I see, in that case we'd better hurry. Lead the way, Shaky!'

Shaky moved at such an impressive speed that Delia had trouble keeping up with him. They were only a few metres outside the garden when they found Milton. He was lying motionless. Delia flapped her wings, gently hitting him in the face. 'Milton! Can you hear me? Wake up! *Please* wake up, Milton.'

'Is he alive?' asked Shaky. 'Is he going to be alright?'

'I'm not sure. Do you know what happened to him?'

'I've no idea. This is how I found him. I would have walked straight past if it wasn't for the awful smell.'

Delia pressed her ears to his mouth and listened to his breathing. She could feel his warm breath against her beak and see his chest moving. For a moment, his eyes opened.

'Milton. It's Delia. Don't worry, you're going to be alright; we're here now. Can you tell me what happened?'

'Water,' he said 'I need some water.'

'Back in a moment!' said Shaky.

After a few minutes he returned, balancing a flower head full of water on his head. 'Here you go.' He tried to pour the water carefully into Milton's mouth, but couldn't help spilling some onto his head.

After just a few minutes, Delia had calmed her nerves and was busy cleaning the wound on his foot. Then she began to splint his other leg with a small twig and tied the whole thing together neatly with some hair donated from Shaky's tail.

'I had a fight,' said Milton, wearily.

'A *fight*? With *whom*?'

'And what on earth for?' Said Shaky.

'It was the Tabby cat from Hannah's house. She wanted to kill me.'

'And almost did from the look of you,' said Delia.

'I think she was hurt more than me. I only went over there to impress Hannah at her party.'

'What party?' said Delia.

'The one you told April about. Surely you remember!... It was only yesterday.'

'I'm quite sure I don't know what you're talking about. Did you bang your head during the fight?'

'Err... no. I guess she must have made a mistake then.'

'I think you need to talk to April,' said Shaky. 'In the meantime let's get you back into the garden.'

Later that afternoon Milton sat tending to his wounds next to the pond. The sun was still bright enough to warm the water, and it soothed his foot nicely. The sparkle in the water helped his headache too. He was just closing his eyes to block out the pain from his other leg, when April landed next to him.

'Hello, Milton.'

'Guess what happened to me,' he said, raising his foot from the water.

April looked down at her feet and began to cry.

'I have a confession,' she said, sobbing. 'I've betrayed you, Milton, and I don't think you will ever forgive me.'

'What on earth are you saying?'

'I don't know how to explain it. The reason you're hurt; it's all my fault!'

She continued to sob and couldn't look Milton in the eyes. 'I helped the cat. I helped her to get you alone. I *knew* there was no party and *I* sent you there. *I* sent you to be killed!'

He frowned and his mouth dropped open, he couldn't believe his ears. This was April. *This was April.*

'Why would you do that? I thought we were friends. I thought we were best friends!'

'It wasn't that easy, she was going to kill my babies. She was going to kill them all.'

'Why didn't you just tell me?'

'What good would that have done? I couldn't see a way out. There wasn't time. I was alone. I had to choose between my best friend and hundreds of my defenceless children.'

'I would still have gone. I would have gone and fought the cat for *you*, April... to save your children. *Friends* make sacrifices for each other. At least I would have been prepared for the fight.'

'I'm *so* sorry, Milton. I don't expect you to ever forgive me.'

He turned back towards the pond and dipped his sore foot back into the water.

'Just go away,' he said. 'I want to be alone.'

April crawled away, still sobbing. He could see from the corner of his eye that she was looking back from the edge of the garden, willing him to look. He kept his back to her.

Chapter 13 - Boar Meets Sow

The garden became chilly later in the evening but looked much warmer because of an amber red glow from the low sunlight. Milton had fallen asleep from exhaustion with his feet still dipped in the water. His toes had wrinkled up in the pond. A light breeze blew through the garden sending a shiver up his spine which woke him up. When he rubbed the sleep from his eyes, he noticed a pile of food next to him. There was a slug, a worm, two mushrooms and a host of grass roots. He was confused, and looked around for an explanation. Perhaps April was trying to make up with him. It would take more than a few bugs. He had been betrayed, and he was angry.

He continued to look around. Standing behind him was *another* hedgehog with pale skin, long eyelashes, deep pearly black eyes; clearly a sow, a female. She gracefully moved closer to him.

'Hello, handsome,' she said, 'I thought you could do with some food. You look *awfully* thin for this time of the year. You really ought to be fattening up for winter; it won't be long before all the food runs out, you know.'

'Thanks for the advice. It's nice to have someone looking out for *me* for a change. I'm Milton by the way.'

'I know. Delia told me all about you and your adventures here. I just *had* to see the famous acrobatic hedgehog for myself. I'm Faith.'

He blushed and realized he was gazing like a love-sick puppy dog. Faith was attractive and stunning.

'*Faith*,' he said, smiling. 'What a beautiful name.'

Faith told stories about her journey to the garden from a riverbank over three days walk away.

'I was afraid I might run into a fox,' she said. 'My mother warned me about them.'

'Don't worry, I'll protect you. I'm not afraid of being killed by a fox. I just hope I'm not there if it happens.'

The hours seemed to pass by in minutes when they were together. While she talked, he studied her like she was a fine artwork. Every detail of her features seemed radiant and elegant at the same time. She described her ambition in life to raise a family, and something connected between them. It was like they had known each other all their lives.

He felt as if a hole had grown deep inside his soul, and he knew only she would be able to fill it. Everything now seemed clear; his purpose in life was unclouded. Destiny had helped him survive, and now it had brought him and Faith together.

Whenever something wonderful like this happened, he desperately wanted to share the news with his father. It was times like these that he missed him the most. He would have loved to meet her.

Before long it was morning; they had been talking all night, and were now nestled comfortably side by side with each other.

'Sweet dreams,' she said, kissing his forehead. He was already fast asleep.

Chapter 14 - Destiny

The Robinson's house had never been so busy. The Watt's had been invited over for dinner, and everyone came. Mr Watt and Mr Robinson were sitting in the living room – half-watching the television, eating biscuits and talking about golf. Mrs Watt was helping out in the kitchen making some coffee, while Mrs Robinson attended to the dinner boiling on the stove. Hannah and Robert were setting the dining table.

'Hannah,' called Mrs Robinson, through the hatch. 'Go and play with your brother in the garden. Dinner won't be ready for a while yet.'

Robert stole a ribbon from Hannah's hair, chuckled, and galloped out of the patio doors into the garden. It was the first time he had been allowed out of the house, since his father caught him hitting the cat.

Mr Watt had once worked for a pet rescue charity and despised animal cruelty of any kind. He would never hurt his children that wouldn't teach them anything, but he was very firm. He had, instead, taken away everything Robert cared about. He took his television, computer, posters, stereo, action figures, everything. He even took the duvet from his bed and replaced it with an itchy blanket. All of Robert's treasures were locked in the attic, until he had done enough housework to earn them back. It took a month, but he learned his lesson.

Hannah left Robert, and ran to the end of the garden in search of Milton. She peeled back the hedgerow behind the garden shed and found him nesting with Faith.

The initial surprise of seeing two hedgehogs confused an expression of joy with sadness. Hannah immediately began thinking about her recent break up with Adam. At least *Milton* had found love.

The two hedgehogs opened their eyes to see her peering down at them.

'I'm glad you've found someone, Milton. You look adorable together. I hope *I* find someone like that one day.'

Hannah's approval sealed Milton's own feelings. There was no doubt when he looked at Faith that something wonderful had begun.

'Take a look at this!' shouted Robert, waving her ribbon in the air like a wizard. Totally surrounding him was a magic whirlwind of tiny red ladybirds, fluttering in formation while he danced in a circle.

Hannah ran across and joined in with the spectacle, laughing with excitement. One of the ladybirds was a little larger than the rest and hovered across to where Milton and Faith were sitting.

'Good afternoon,' said April, nervously.

'Don't worry,' said Milton. 'Forgiveness is the food of friendship, and I forgive you.'

'I'm truly sorry,' said April, sincerely. 'I *won't* let you down again.'

'Congratulations,' said Faith. 'You must be so proud of your little babies.'

'I am. I *really* am!'

'Hey, listen,' said Milton. 'What did the hedgehog say when it backed into a cactus? Is that *you*, Mum?'

April chuckled. She knew it would take time to earn his trust again, but was pleased to have the chance. She flew back to her flock, much happier.

Hannah and Robert danced around the garden, until dinner was ready, and then hurried inside with hungry bellies.

Milton took a deep breath and huddled closer to Faith and said, 'Well, I'm finally an uncle.'

'Milton,' said Faith, smiling. 'I think I might be pregnant.'

The End

Lightning Source UK Ltd.
Milton Keynes UK
13 November 2009

146202UK00001BA/8/P